D1310091

Presented to

Lisa Perez (Sister of my heart!)

By

Sue

On the Occasion of

Thanksgiving 84M

Date 1-17-08

Lets do this

healthy lifestyle

together! :)

COME SIT AWHILE

The JOYS OF FRIENDSHIP AND LOVE

INSPIRATION *from the* FRONT PORCH

by Roy Lessin & Heather Solum

BARBOUR
PUBLISHING

Cover design by Greg Jackson, Jackson Design Co, llc

Cover and interior art by Barbara Pascolini

Published by Barbour Publishing, Inc., P.O. Box 719, Uhrichsville, Ohio 44683, www.barbourbooks.com

Our mission is to publish and distribute inspirational products offering exceptional value and biblical encouragement to the masses.

 Member of the
Evangelical Christian
Publishers Association

Printed in China.
5 4 3 2 1

The *Come Sit Awhile* gift book series is a
collection of heartwarming stories, scriptures,
recipes, quotes, prayers, and inspirational
thoughts of hope and encouragement. We have
chosen the theme of the front porch because it not
only speaks of a place where people gather, relax,
and enjoy the pleasures of each other's company,
but it is also symbolic of a special place in our
hearts where rest is found, where we enjoy the
sweetness of God's presence, and where priceless
memories are gathered and cherished always.

Abraham. . .

was called the Friend of God.

JAMES 2:23 KJV

The brilliance of a full moon, the fragrance of honeysuckle, the music of crickets and frogs, the flashes of fireflies, the clean smell of the air after a summer storm, the darting of a hummingbird as it gathers nectar, the laughter of children playing in the distance, the secrets shared between best friends on the porch swing, the warmth of unspoken love that surrounds you. . . These are only a few of the simple pleasures found by those who spend time on the front porch.

Sleeping Out

I have many special memories from my growing-up years on the farm. One of those special memories is the experience of sleeping out on our screened-in front porch. The only disappointment I experienced was on those nights when, during a storm, lightning came too close to the porch, and I had to gather my bedding and come into the house. . . .

The porch was on the west side of our gabled farmhouse and faced the rolling grain fields of our neighbors. The only piece of furniture on our porch was an old coiled-spring bed. Most of the year the porch was unused, but in the warm days of summer, that porch became my treasured place. My heart will always remember the joys I found there—the wonder of gazing at the star-filled heavens, the delight of the soothing sound of chirping crickets, the over-whelming beauty of lightning flashes from a distant thunderstorm, and the pleasure of the company of a girlfriend as we laughed and talked long into the night.

CHARLENE LESSIN

The shade provided by a porch brings great relief as we seek shelter from the strong rays of the summer sun. God's loving presence is also our protective covering, providing us with needed relief and shelter from the trials and difficulties of life.

YOU HAVE BEEN
A REFUGE FOR THE POOR,
A REFUGE FOR THE NEEDY
IN HIS DISTRESS,
A SHELTER FROM THE STORM
AND A SHADE FROM THE HEAT.

ISAIAH 25:4 NIV

There are front porches and back porches. . .
side porches and wraparound porches. . .
screened-in porches and open porches. . .
country porches and city porches. . .lake porches
and ocean porches. . .

The important thing about a porch is not its
size, type, or location, but its usage. Porches
need people to pass by, to walk through, and to
sit down and linger awhile.

*A porch is
so hospitable that
even a pair of
dirty boots can find
a welcome place to land.*

The best meal you can enjoy on a porch is when love is passed from heart to heart to heart.

Orange Slice Bars

4 eggs	1 teaspoon baking
2 ½ cups brown	powder
sugar	⅛ teaspoon salt
1 teaspoon vanilla	16 orange slice candies,
2 ¼ cups flour	cut up
	½ cup nutmeats (walnuts)

Beat eggs well. Add the sugar; stir well. Add vanilla. Sift together the flour, baking powder, and salt. Add the rest of mixture. Stir in the cut-up orange slice candies and the nutmeats (walnuts). Spread on a greased 11x16-inch jelly roll pan. Bake for 15–20 minutes at 350°. Cut into squares while hot. (Finely chopped sunflower seeds can also be used on these bars. Sprinkle seeds on top before bars are put into the oven.)

MRS. LOUIS LARSON

LOVE

NEVER FAILS.

1 CORINTHIANS 13:8 NIV

WHEN OUR HEARTS ARE HEAVY,

    love comforts us;

WHEN OUR HEARTS ARE FEARFUL,

    love assures us;

WHEN OUR HEARTS ARE ANXIOUS,

    love quiets us;

WHEN OUR HEARTS ARE RESTLESS,

    love keeps us;

WHEN OUR HEARTS ARE TROUBLED,

    love calms us;

WHEN OUR HEARTS ARE
DOWNCAST,

    love lifts us.

    LOVE NEVER FAILS.

The front porch provides the perfect climate for visiting, sharing, listening, and caring.

————————

Love turns a house into a home. . . .
Grace turns a home into a haven.

Then those who

feared and loved the Lord

spoke often of him to each other.

And he had a Book of Remembrance

drawn up in which he recorded

the names of those who

feared him and loved to think about him.

MALACHI 3:16 TLB

PLEASANT WORDS ARE
AS AN HONEYCOMB,
SWEET TO THE SOUL,
AND HEALTH TO THE BONES.

PROVERBS 16:24 KJV

THERE'S A BLESSING
IN THE SUNSHINE,
AND IN THE MORNING DEW.
BUT ONE OF
MY GREATEST BLESSINGS
IS THE TIME I SPEND
WITH YOU.

esus said to those who followed Him, "I have called you friends." Think of it—the God of creation wants to have a personal relationship with us. God delights in being with us person to person, heart to heart, friend to friend. In His presence there truly is fullness of joy and pleasure forevermore. What better company could we possibly keep?

*H*ow good and how pleasant it is for brethren to dwell together in unity! It is like the precious ointment upon the head, that ran down upon the beard, even Aaron's beard: that went down to the skirts of his garments; as the dew of Hermon, and as the dew that descended upon the mountains of Zion: for there the LORD commanded the blessing, even life for evermore.

PSALM 133:1–3 KJV

Aunt Jane's Hot Dish

(This comfort dish tastes great with potato chips.)

1 pound ground beef
1 cup chopped onion
1½ cups diced celery
2 cans cream of mushroom or
    cream of celery soup
1 cup white rice
2 tablespoons soy sauce
½ cup water

Brown ground beef with onion. Drain. Add
celery and remaining ingredients. Mix together
in casserole dish and bake at 350° for 1½ hours.
Stir once during baking time.

God has given you another day—

    to hear His voice,

        to see His face,

            to enjoy His company,

                to walk in His ways,

            to delight in His presence,

        to discover His goodness,

    to embrace His love.

What a day this will be!

No one can
place a price tag on
the value of
a praying friend.

A FRIEND LOVES
AT ALL TIMES.

PROVERBS 17:17 NKJV

The Things You Find in a Friend

A caring way, a winning smile,

A willingness to go the extra mile;

A giving heart, a radiant glow,

A thoughtfulness that helps you grow;

A listening ear, a servant's way,

A special bond that's felt each day.

*A porch light is
a very welcome sight.*

The breadth of God's love reaches into

every need and circumstance of your life. . . .

The length of His love is unfailing and will

faithfully guide your way. . . .

The height of His love will raise you up and

lift you out of every valley. . . .

The depth of His love will daily draw you closer

to His heart.

A FRONT PORCH IS

A GREAT MEMORY MAKER.

When you count your blessings,

the number multiplies

when you count a friend.

Turn, O LORD, and deliver me;

save me because of your unfailing love.

PSALM 6:4 NIV

We can look up to God, because His love will

never let us down.

THE TRUE MEASURE

OF LOVE IS

TO LOVE WITHOUT MEASURE!

ST. BERNARD

May you daily be. . .

Kept in God's perfect peace;

Blessed with His matchless grace;

Assured of His caring presence;

Sheltered by His awesome greatness;

Covered with His steadfast love.

Neighbors are so special,

They bring blessings without end;

Especially when your neighbors

Turn out to be dear friends.

The love of God

covers you on every side,

in every direction,

inside and out,

over and under,

in front and behind.

The impact of
a true friend upon your life
is something that words
can never fully express
and something that your heart
can never fully measure.

*B*e persuaded, that neither death with its

voice of fear, nor life with its many cares, nor the

attacks of the enemy which falsely accuse you,

nor things present with their pressing claims, nor

things to come with their dark shadows, nor the

height of any mountains that stand in your way,

nor the depths of a great trial that you may walk

through, nor any person or circumstance which

tries to quench your joy or rob you of your peace

shall be able to move you away,

by even a single inch,

from the love of God

that covers and

guards your life.

PARAPHRASE OF
ROMANS 8:38-39

[LOVE] ALWAYS PROTECTS,

ALWAYS TRUSTS,

ALWAYS HOPES,

ALWAYS PERSEVERES.

LOVE NEVER FAILS.

1 CORINTHIANS 13:7–8 NIV

I love to visit with a friend on my front porch in the early evening, when dusk transitions into nightfall. It is the perfect time of day to sit on our porch rockers and talk, as the stars begin to fill up the night sky. The conversation often varies between family, food, and the things that God is doing in our lives. One thing I especially enjoy is the unhurried atmosphere the porch creates as my friend and I enjoy the pleasure of each other's company.

God is a
loving, forgiving,
restoring, embracing,
caring, faithful
Father.

There is no place

beyond God's strength. . .

no boundaries to His love. . .

no limit to His mercies. . .

no shortage of His grace.

He responds to us with

loving-kindness and

a multitude of tender mercies.

One day
you will be amazed
to discover the many ways
God has used your life
to be a blessing to others.

The impact of one life

upon another can bring

change, comfort, hope, encouragement,

and many other influences for good—

all of which will make an eternal difference.

It is in our times of
deepest need that we find the depths
to which the tenderness
and grace of Jesus can reach.
For who alone but Jesus can bring us comfort
and assurance with His all-
embracing love.

There's something special

about creating a

new memory with

an old friend.

THE FOOTPRINTS OF
A FRIEND WILL
FOLLOW YOU INTO THE VALLEYS
AS WELL AS
ONTO THE MOUNTAINTOPS.

When you don't feel that

   you have to be perfect to be accepted. . .

When you are given the freedom

   to be yourself in every situation. . .

When you can ask for an opinion

   knowing you'll be given the truth. . .

When you can share your heart

   without the risk of betrayal. . .

When being together is

   more important than what you do. . .

That is when you know that

   you are in the company

   of a friend.

God made us dependent on each other. Even though He is with us and in us, He does not want us to walk alone. We need each other to grow, to be supported in prayer, to express the Father's love, to comfort one another, and to know the Shepherd's care. We need each other to be formed in character, to be encouraged in our fight of faith, and to persevere until that day when all our needs shall be fully met when we see Him.

God's "One Another" Family

So we, being many, are one body in Christ,

and every one members one of another.

ROMANS 12:5 KJV

———————

God has given every true believer in Jesus

Christ a membership in His family. In His family,

each member belongs to one another and needs

one another. Your "one another" family is bigger

than you could ever dream. You belong to the

family of God around the world. . .and they

belong to you.

God has made us dependent upon one

another. We have a built-in need for the fellow-
ship, prayer, support, encouragement, and help of
others in God's family. God wants us to come
to Him in prayer, but He also wants us to pray
for one another. God loves us deeply and per-
sonally, but He often expresses His love to us
through others. Think of all the times you have
felt God's touch through the hands of others,
heard God's voice through the words of others,
sensed God's comfort
through the support of
others, and known
God's provision through
the gifts of others.

Marked by Love

Growing up as a little girl, I took in the sights, sounds, and stories that I experienced on my grandma's front porch. I would often sit with her—her right foot keeping the motion of the swing going, her left foot tucked under, while my small feet dangled and moved with the rhythm and creak of the swing chain. My grandmother had the best view of life from her front porch swing. I learned many lessons of love as she reached out and touched so many lives in our neighborhood. On summer evenings we would sit and swing while friendly neighbors would come by, perch on the steps, and talk about their day or family. People in cars driving by would often toot their horns and wave. . . .

My grandmother learned to love others because of the love her mother and father showed

to strangers. As a little girl, Grandmother lived within a short distance of the railroad tracks. She would help her mother watch for hobos who rode in the boxcars of the trains that went by. (Grandmother was always told that hobos were people who had fallen on hard times.) When a hobo would wander the street looking for "food for work," Grandmother's house was often a place where they could chop wood, clean the shed, or wash windows for a home-cooked meal. If there wasn't work to be done, the meal would be given freely. It used to be said that if a hobo found a home where kindness was extended, he would leave a mark near the house that other hobos could identify. If that is true, I'm sure my grandmother's home carried that special mark of love.

ANN BRANDT

GRACE. . .fills our lives with good things;
GRACE. . .is a gift from above—
GRACE. . .fills our home with beauty;
GRACE. . .fills our hearts with love.

Hands to Serve

My hands can serve as He served—

to raise someone who has fallen. . .

to support someone who is weak. . .

to uphold someone who is weary;

to wipe a tear. . .

to hold a hand. . .

to give a cup of water. . .

to embrace a friend. . .

to carry a burden. . .

to impart a blessing. . .

Lord, use my hands.

Deeds of kindness, done in love,

    Diamonds are in settings rare;

In the realms of bliss above

    These the gems the blessed wear.

Let us cherish them with care,

    Looks and words and deeds of love,

Each the other's burden bear,

    Traveling to our home above.

SONG GARDEN

Because God is love,

there is grace;

and because there is grace,

there is hope;

and because there is hope,

we can put a song into our day,

faith into our prayers,

joy into our obedience,

and love into our actions.

*I*n our own strength,

we can only do so much;

in our own wisdom,

we can only know so much;

in our own love,

we can only give so much.

Jesus Christ said that He came to give us life,

and He gives it to us in

overwhelming generosity and abundance.

He wants us to daily focus on His resources,

not on our limitations.

As a little girl, I often spent a week with my grandparents on their farm in rural Minnesota. I have fond memories of those childhood days. My grandparents had a porch where they slept in the summertime because it was cooler than inside the house. The porch was completely surrounded by windows. My bed was also on the porch. I loved lying in my bed at night and looking out at the bright stars. I would drift off to sleep while listening to my grandparents quietly sharing the news and thoughts of their day and their plans for the next.

On my grandparents' porch, there was a swing attached to the ceiling. As children we were told, "Don't swing too high," because it would hit the wall if we did. My favorite time on the swing was with my grandfather. We would sit together in the evenings on the porch and swing while my grand-mother was finishing her chores—cleaning the strawberries she'd picked and gently placing the eggs she'd gathered from the henhouse into the egg cartons to sell. Sometimes my grandpa and I would play a game as we would swing; and at times he would tell me stories from the past. But often we would just sit quietly, delighting in each other's love—it was my favorite time. As I grew older, these times were especially precious to me because of the knowledge of my grandfather's deep faith in the Lord. His silence spoke volumes as he continually grew in his love and faith in Jesus.

DEBBIE HALL

The heart of God will always move you

on to new vistas of His goodness,

new treasures of His grace,

new understanding of His purposes,

and new discoveries of His love.

He will do it with the beauty of His presence,

with the affirmation of His promises,

with the hand of His blessing,

and with the endless assurance of His love.

PARAPHRASE OF EPHESIANS 1:17–18

GOD'S BLESSINGS
ARE ENDLESS;
HIS GRACE
IS MEASURELESS;
AND HIS LOVE
IS MATCHLESS.

God's love is beneath you,

above you, around you, upon you,

within you, behind you, and before you.

It fills every moment of your life

and will embrace you

through all of eternity.

That Christ may dwell

in your hearts through faith; that you,

being rooted and grounded in love,

may be able to comprehend

with all the saints what is

the width and length and depth and height—

to know the love of Christ

which passes knowledge;

that you may be filled with

all the fullness of God.

EPHESIANS 3:17–19 NKJV

God is thinking about you at this very moment. He's not just thinking one thought but more thoughts than you can count.

God's mind is filled with thoughts about you because His heart is filled with love for you.

Blessed is that man

*who makes the L*ORD *his trust. . . .*

*Many, O L*ORD *my God,*

are Your wonderful works

Which You have done;

And Your thoughts toward us

Cannot be recounted to You in order;

If I would declare and speak of them,

They are more than can be numbered.

PSALM 40:4–5 NKJV

When God speaks to us about His hands,

He wants us to recognize His power;

When He speaks to us about His face,

He wants us to see His glory;

When He speaks to us about the cross,

He wants us to know His heart.

*H*e opened His arms

to press you to His bosom;

He opened His heart

to welcome you there;

He opened up all

His Divine fullness of life and love,

and offered to take you up

into its fellowship,

to make you wholly one with Himself.

ANDREW MURRAY

God's love is all embracing.

And he arose and came to his father.

But when he was still a great way off,

his father saw him and had compassion,

and ran and fell on his neck and kissed him.

LUKE 15:20 NKJV

God's hand is extended to you like the hand of a close friend. He doesn't reach out to you to keep you at a distance but to draw you close to His heart; not to forbid you access to His love, but to pour it upon you in abundance.

*J*ESUS IS
THE SUNRISE OF YOUR MORNING
AND THE SUNSET OF YOUR DAY.
HIS MERCY WILL
GREET YOU EVERY MORNING,
AND HIS GOODNESS WILL
TUCK YOU IN EACH NIGHT.

*Great is
his faithfulness;
his mercies begin
afresh each day.*

LAMENTATIONS 3:23 NLT

*L*oved with everlasting love,

　　Led by grace that love to know;

Spirit, breathing from above,

　　Thou hast taught me it is so!

Oh, this full and perfect peace!

　　Oh, this transport all divine!

In a love which cannot cease,

　　I am His, and He is mine.

G. WADE ROBINSON

The Lord wants you to rest in His love. His love will never fail you. Everything that is good in your life has been started by Him, is sustained by Him, and will be completed by Him. He is involved in every detail of your life.

I know whom I have believed
and am persuaded that He
is able to keep what I have
committed to Him until that Day.

2 TIMOTHY 1:12 NKJV

I am sure that God,
who began the good work within you,
will continue his work until it is finally finished
on that day when Christ Jesus comes back again.

PHILIPPIANS 1:6 NLT

"No longer do I call you servants,

for a servant does not know

what his master is doing;

but I have called you friends,

for all things that I heard from My Father

I have made known to you."

JOHN 15:15 NKJV

*G*od wants us to continue to grow in Him because there are—

MORE MOMENTS TO DELIGHT IN

than we've enjoyed,

MORE BLESSINGS TO HAVE

than we've received,

MORE LOVE TO EMBRACE

than we've experienced.

The LORD has appeared

of old to me, saying:

"Yes, I have loved you

with an everlasting love;

Therefore with lovingkindness

I have drawn you."

JEREMIAH 31:3 NKJV

God's love for you never runs out or dries up. He doesn't love you on your good days and cease loving you on your bad days. He loved you even before you were born. "Everlasting love" not only refers to the length of time that God has loved you, but it also refers to the quality of His love. There is nothing shallow to be found in God's everlasting love. It is out of the depths of His love that He drew your heart to His.

*L*ove expressed itself in many heartfelt ways from our front porch on the family farm. The porch was open and large and offered a spectacular view of the countryside. One of my favorite things to gaze upon was my mother's flower garden. Oak trees, lilac bushes, rocks, and a white picket fence bordered it. The garden's brilliant blooms were testimonies to my mother's yearly labor of love in that special place. . . .

The porch contained a two-seated platform swing (seats facing each other), and a large, overstuffed rocking chair. I had two younger brothers. When my youngest brother was born, I would often bundle him up in a warm quilt and carry him to the front-porch rocker. There we would sit, rocking back and forth in the cool, crisp autumn air until he would fall asleep in my arms. My other brother and I shared many happy times on that platform swing. We spent countless hours laughing and swinging, enjoying the simple pleasures of childhood that our loving home provided.

C.R.L.

PERFECT LOVE IS NOT
A FEELING YOU HAVE
BUT A PERSON THAT
YOUR HEART
COMES TO KNOW.

"Always" is a word that fits God perfectly. God is eternal, and every attribute and aspect of His nature is eternal. He has always been who He is now, and who He is now is who He will always be. All that He has been to you, He is and will always be. God is love, was love, and always will be love. He is good, was good, and will always be good. He was faithful, is faithful, and will always be faithful.

Think of the loving ways that

Jesus speaks of His relationship to you:

Groom to the bride,

Brother to a brother,

Friend to a friend.

Having Jesus call you His friend doesn't mean a casual, informal friendship, but rather a deep, intimate friendship. Every quality that we desire in a best friend is found in our relationship with Him. Jesus abides with us, walks with us, and speaks His heart to us. He is completely trustworthy, loyal, and true. He is always there for you; He gives you His complete attention; He cares about your needs; and He loves you unconditionally.

*G*od wants you to experience His "alls,"

not just "portions."

He wants to give you all of the grace you will need,

not just a portion.

He wants you to receive all spiritual blessings,

not just a portion.

He wants to fill all of your heart with His love,

not just a portion.

Praise to the Lord,

who with marvelous wisdom

hath made thee!

Decked thee with health,

and with loving hand

guided and stayed thee;

How oft in grief

Hath not He brought thee relief,

Spreading His wings

for to shade thee!

JOACHIM NEANDER

Your love, Lord, Oh Your love—

Like a flower unfolding,

Like strong arms upholding,

Your love strengthens me.

Your love, Lord, Oh Your love—

Like words unending,

Like prayers ascending,

Your love nurtures me.

Your love, Lord, Oh Your love —

Like rivers cascading,

Like the oak tree's shading,

Your love shelters me.

Your love, Lord, Oh Your love —

Like wings that are soaring,

Like dew in the morning,

Your love covers me.

God's love is

Too great to comprehend;

Too awesome to be replaced;

Too high to climb its summit;

Too wide for arms to embrace.

No patriot ever loved his country;

no mother ever loved her baby;

no father ever loved his boy;

no bridegroom ever loved his bride;

no, not all the love of

all the created beings on this earth

put together would equal the love

which God bears to you.

WILLIAM BOOTH

God was the one who formed you, gave you the breath of life, and brought you into the world. He did this so that His arms could embrace you and His heart could love you. He wants you to know that your relationship with Him is always of more value than the things you do for Him. He wants you to be certain that He loves you completely. He never wants your service for Him to become a way of trying to earn His love. The reason that you don't have to earn His love is because you already have it.

GOD'S BANNER OVER YOU
IS LOVE—
WALK UNDER IT;
RALLY AROUND IT;
WRAP YOURSELF IN IT!

Jesus has called you to come to Him

and abide with Him.

"Come" is the cord of love;

"Abide" the band of love

which holds you fast.

ANDREW MURRAY

WHENEVER YOU PRAY,

it is the Father's heart of love that responds to you.

WHENEVER YOU FALL,

it is His hands of love that lift you up.

WHENEVER YOU ARE TROUBLED,

it is His embrace of love that comforts you.

WHENEVER YOU ARE DISCOURAGED,

it is His voice of love that encourages you.

WHENEVER YOU ARE INSECURE,

it is His smile of love that reassures you.

WHENEVER YOU ARE HURTING,

it is His touch of love that makes you whole.

$\mathcal{D}$ear friends, let us continue to love one another, for love comes from God. Anyone who loves is born of God and knows God. But anyone who does not love does not know God—for God is love. God showed how much he loved us by sending his only Son into the world so that we might have eternal life through him. This is real love. It is not that we loved God, but that he

loved us and sent his Son as a sacrifice to take away our sins.

1 JOHN 4:7–10 NLT